The Love Story of
REDEMPTION

Redemption, Rest, Rejoice in Jesus

Kay F. Dimeo

The Love Story of Redemption
© 2023 Reverend Kay F Dimeo BSc MA. All rights reserved.

No part of this book may be reproduced in any form or
by any means, electronic, mechanical, digital, photocopying or
recording, except for the inclusion in a review, without
permission in writing from the publisher.

ISBN 978-1-66640-619-1

Book & cover design by Darlene Swanson • www.van-garde.com

Contents

Chapter One

The Love Story of Redemption

God loves you so much that He gave His only Son to bring you back from destruction and make you His own. Redemption is a love story.

The concept of redemption is pivotal throughout the time of God's relationship with the whole of humanity.

'Redeemed' is used over 50 times in the Bible. 20 of these are in the New Testament. 'Redemption' is used over 230 times throughout scripture.

In the Old Testament there are laws given by God to the nation of Hebrews telling of the way to live in all manner of circumstances. These are for safety, wellbeing, and hygiene. The Hebrews called these scriptures the Torah.

Laws were laid down to direct people as to how they should handle situations such as loss of family members and family members suffering impoverishment. There should be help given from individuals and from the whole community.

Those who had the task of helping were referred to as redeemers.

> *If a fellow countryman of yours becomes*
> *so poor he has to sell part of his property,*
> *then his nearest kinsman is to come and*
> *redeem what his brother has sold.*
>
> *Leviticus 25:25-28*

> *If brothers are living together and one*
> *of them dies without a son his widow*
> *must not marry outside the family. Her*
> *husband's brother shall take her and*

*marry her and fulfil the duty
of a brother-in-law to her.*

Deuteronomy 25:5

Thus, we have the name of the rescuer, Kinsman Redeemer.

We find the story of a Kinsman Redeemer in the book of Ruth. It is the compelling story of faithfulness, devotion, and love. The story is of Naomi, Ruth and Ruth's Kinsman Redeemer, Boaz.

The story is set in the land of Galilee in the town of Bethlehem. Bethlehem was Jesus Christ's, birthplace. It was foretold that Jesus was to be born there.

*"But you, Bethlehem Ephrathah, though
you are small among the clans of Judah,
out of you will come for me one who will
be ruler over Israel, whose origins are from
of old, from ancient times."*

Micah 5:2

The story is placed during the time of the Judges, 6th to 4th century BC, that is before the Hebrew people chose to have a king. At that time the nation was a theocracy, led and governed by God alone. Later they became a nation governed by a king, rather than be governed by God alone, their first king was King Saul. You can read about that changeover in the book of Samuel.

Naomi and her husband, Elimelech and their two sons, Mahlon and Chilion left Bethlehem. They then settled in Moab. Nothing is said as to why they left Bethlehem, but Moab and Israel were friendly at that time.

Time passed and the sons married Moabite women Ruth and Orpah. More time passed then Elimelech, Mahlon and Chilion passed away. This left Naomi and her two daughters-in-law, both of whom were childless.

Naomi decided to return to Bethlehem.

For women to be left without husbands meant that, in most cases, they were left without the money to live. If the widow did not have any offspring, it became the duty of a family member to marry the widow and continue the heritage of the dead man's inheritance.

Naomi sold a field during this time of penury; she needed money to live.

Naomi told Orpah and Ruth to go back to their own people for help. Orpah said she would, but Ruth was emphatic in her determination to stay with Naomi. Ruth had adopted Naomi's religion as her own and she loved her dearly.

> *"And Ruth said, Intreat me not to leave thee, or to return from following after thee: for whither thou goest, I will go; and where thou lodgest, I will lodge: thy people shall be my people, and thy God my God:"*
>
> *Ruth 1:16*

Naomi returned to Bethlehem with her daughter-in-law, Ruth. It was the time of the barley harvest.

It was the custom in the Hebrew culture to let people take what they needed from the edges of the fields, this was to help the poor and save them from starving. Ruth went to the fields to collect barley. She was noticed by the owner of the field, Boaz, and he told his workers to let her take what she needed, and they were not to harm her in anyway. Boaz had heard of Ruth's virtuosity, how she had devoted herself to

Naomi and how she had taken Naomi's religion as her own.

Naomi told Ruth that Boaz was indeed a close relative.

Under the cover of darkness Ruth waited until Boaz woke from sleep to ask him to fulfil the responsibilities of a kinsman redeemer. To marry her. Boaz replied that there was another man who was a closer relative, and he would talk to him first. They waited until it was almost light, and Ruth left before anyone could recognise her.

It's not difficult to imagine the excitement taking place in both Naomi's house and in Boaz's heart. What mounting tension must have been going on as the possibilities were being talked of. This man's care, making sure her shawl was full of ephahs of barley. And sending her home in the darkness before dawn before she could be recognised. All this would be discussed.

In the end the other close relative did not want to fulfil his obligations and it was resolved that Boaz should marry Ruth and save both Ruth and Naomi.

Boaz married Ruth.

So, there we are,

Ruth, a Moabitess, through tragic circumstances came to be living in Bethlehem where she met Boaz: A pagan women from Moab who adopted the Hebrew religion and became a forebear of Jesus, our Saviour. She was the great grandmother of King David. She was indeed redeemed, redeemed from living a Godless life to being a God-fearing women blessed by God by having her name written in the books of history as a testament to God's saving grace.

The book of Ruth is read during the Jewish holiday of Shavuot.

Boaz foreshadows Jesus Christ, the ultimate kinsman redeemer, who will redeem all His people. The story of Ruth portrays God's loving kindness and blessing on the righteous. He drew Ruth into His own family, the Hebrew nation, and blessed her with a child who would be a forebear of Christ. In the same way throughout history God has been drawing people to himself, calling them to turn from their sins and their wicked ways and to live in union with Him in a righteous life. Believing for an eternity in Christ.

In the Old Testament messengers were sent to the people to tell them of the change needed to become one of God's own family. These men and women were prophets such as Ezekiel, Isaiah, Daniel, Amos, Habakkuk and Deborah.

God saw that the problem with people was that they reverted to disobedience. Even although they repent, they often turned back to sin as in the days of Moses when the people made a golden calf to worship. They sought forgiveness for doing this but not long after they were complaining against God for their difficulties in the desert. So, their initial repentance was not enough to bring about a complete change. Their hearts needed to be changed. They needed a new heart. A heart that belonged solely to God that the first commandment may be obeyed: Love the Lord your God with all your heart and all your soul and with all your mind.

"You shall love the Lord your God with all your heart and with all your soul and with all your mind and with all your strength" (Mark 12:30). This, the greatest commandment, calls us to love God with our whole being. We are to be vigorous in every one of our faculties, cultivating devotion to God. Heart, soul, strength, and mind.

But we all, like sheep, have gone away Isaiah says:

We all, like sheep, have gone astray,
each of us has turned to our own way;
and the LORD has laid on him the iniquity
of us all.

Isaiah 53:6

We need a redeemer; Jesus is His name.

Jesus addresses a different human condition, the condition of the heart.

Because it is so easy to go astray a deeper work is needed and only Jesus could achieve that deeper work, it is done through the cross and the shedding of His blood.

"Ye were redeemed, not with corruptible
things, with silver or gold, from your vain
manner of life handed down from your
fathers; but with precious blood, as of a
lamb without blemish and without spot,
even the blood of Christ."

1 Peter 1:18

The imbedded sin was handed down to us by our fathers. The origin of sin in our lives is from the death that entered in in the garden of Eden. Adam was disobedient to God and ate the fruit of the tree of knowledge of good and evil. That was rebellion against God and rebellion against God has been happening ever since.

Throughout the generations our fathers have disobeyed and handed down godlessness.

We may argue about how sinful we are, for example we may compare ourselves with others, thinking "I am not bad, God will accept me as I am." "I have never hurt anyone." But that is because we are not honest, we are quick to forget what we have in fact done. We may think "I didn't mean to do that; that was not my intention, I will not do that again". But it happens again, and you have no power over it. Only Jesus can break that stronghold in your life. Only Jesus, because Jesus is pure and spotless, only He could take away the sin.

> *"The Lord has laid on Him the
> iniquity of us all"*
>
> *Isaiah 53:6*

We cannot know what happened on the Cross. It is a mystery what happened when Jesus gave up His life, but we do know that He bled and died and took all our sin upon Himself. He became sin for us. He opened the way for us to meet with God. Jesus stood in our place, took our sin, broke the curse that was there from the time of Adam. He redeemed us out of our spiritual poverty, out of the darkness and fear of the future. In Him and by Him we are redeemed, all chains that Satan bound us with are broken.

Jesus, by his death on the cross, by shedding His blood, rescued us from our impoverished state. We can be reconciled with God.

> *"Being justified freely by*
> *his grace through the redemption*
> *that is in Christ."*
>
> *Romans 3:24*

All this was done without cost to the believer. No transaction between ourselves and God is possible, we cannot buy any part of what He did for us, no amount of good works, no number of monetary gifts or donations can buy our redemption. We cannot earn it. It is freely given by God.

A prayer to God

> *Dear Heavenly Father, forgive me*
> *my sin that I may enter the 'rest'*
> *you have promised to those*
> *who trust and obey You.*

Chapter Two
Rest, An Emotional and Spiritual Reset

"The hymn writer Helen Lemmel wrote:

1. O soul are you weary and troubled?
    No light in the darkness you see?
    There's light for a look at the Saviour,
    And life more abundant and free!

    Refrain:
    Turn your eyes upon Jesus,
    Look full in His wonderful face,
    And the things of earth will grow strangely dim,
    In the light of His glory and grace.

Through death into life everlasting
He passed, and we follow Him there;
O'er us sin no more hath dominion—
For more than conqu'rors we are!

His Word shall not fail you—He promised;
Believe Him, and all will be well:
Then go to a world that is dying,
His perfect salvation to tell!

> *"Lord, thou hast made us for thyself, and*
> *our hearts are restless until they find their*
> *rest in Thee".*
> *(Confessions, by Augustine, Book 1).*

Jesus said:

> *"Come unto me, all ye that labour*
> *and are heavy laden, and*
> *I will give you rest"*
> *(Matthew 11.28 KJV).*

A spiritual transaction is made when we admit our sins and iniquities. When we repent and ask Jesus to come into our lives.

Upon declaration of faith, faith in God and His provision for us by sending Jesus to die on the Cross, we enter the Kingdom of Heaven.

The Kingdom of Heaven, the place of rest, is the presence of God, Jesus, and the Holy Spirit. It is also the realm of angels. We have been moved from the darkness into the light: We are now In Christ Jesus and Jesus is in us. What a wonderful thing this is – to be in Christ.

> *"I am the vine; you are the branches. If you remain in me and I in you, you will bear much fruit; apart from me you can do nothing.*
>
> *John 15:5*

A peace and reassurance of sins forgiven emanates from the believer's very core. The world looks brighter, and a new dawn of love shines all around.

To be 'at rest' is to have that:

"Peace that passes all understanding."
Philippians 4:7.

And this serene rest that belongs to those whose consciences are sprinkled in the blood of the One with whom the Father is well pleased will be completed when we meet Jesus face to face.

What happens next? What happens after this moment of conversion? It is, of course, a matter of fact that some people who experience these blessings had previously been immersed in destructive habits and ungodly lifestyles. For example, not being honest with a spouse. Or living with someone without the commitment of marriage. The new Christian may now be in two minds. They may say what happened was very good, but can I change my life that much?

After the conversion experience the devil may whisper "surely that didn't really happen, you must have imagined these things – life is just the same as it always was" or "you know life was comfortable before all this God talk, just go back to the way things were, easier that way."

This is the beginning of the Battle for the Mind. The brain becomes the centre of discussion with oneself and with the enemy of God, Satan. But it is a wonderful truth that the world and Satan do not now have the power to crash in and remove all the Godliness from the convert's life. The new Christian can listen to that inner voice, the Holy Spirit, and seek God's help in overcoming temptations.

Resting in peace can be maintained by trusting in God.

John H. Sammis wrote the song Trust and Obey

1. When we walk with the Lord
   in the light of his word,
   what a glory he sheds on our way!
   While we do his good will,
   he abides with us still,
   and with all who will trust and obey.

   Refrain:
   Trust and obey, for there's no other way
   to be happy in Jesus, but to trust and obey.

2. Not a burden we bear,
   not a sorrow we share,
   but our toil he doth richly repay;
   not a grief or a loss,

not a frown or a cross,
but is blest if we trust and obey. [Refrain]

3. But we never can prove
the delights of his love
until all on the altar we lay;
for the favour he shows,
for the joy he bestows,
are for them who will trust and obey. [Refrain]

4. Then in fellowship sweet
we will sit at his feet,
or we'll walk by his side in the way;
what he says we will do,
where he sends we will go;
never fear, only trust and obey. [Refrain]

The 'Rest' is Guidance

Living in the Rest of the Lord is the only assured way for knowing God's guidance. If you feel a disquiet or as is said a 'check in the spirit'. Take time to think and pray, this may be a warning not to move in a particular direction.

There are others who live in the Kingdom, brothers and sisters who are faithful to God, but there are some who are wolves in sheep's clothing. They pretend to be Godly but inwardly they are vicious, often angry. And want things done their own way.

Again, the still small voice of God will guide you to know who you can trust.

Remain in the place of rest, you will be blessed in so many ways:

> *"No eye has seen; no ear has heard and no mind has imagined what God has prepared for those who love him".*
>
> *1 Corinthians 2:9*

Chapter 3
Rejoice In Sactification

"I am the potter you are the clay".

Jeremiah 18:6

The meaning of sanctification is the action of making or declaring something holy. Believers are holy. They are, as St Paul says, saints. Added to this they are being made holy, made into the image of Christ and ultimately will be completed in holiness when they see Jesus face to face in Heaven. Being made holy is a lifelong process, a journey of discovery – the discovery of God and self-discovery. It is a rich and full life.

Paul said we can be "confident of this very thing, that He who has begun a good work in you will complete it until the day of Jesus Christ" (Philippians 1:6). We might feel marred, disfigured, or flawed, but instead of discarding us, God can reshape us "into another vessel" that is precious and valuable.

Jesus said:

> *"The Spirit of the Lord is upon me,*
> *because he has anointed me*
> *to proclaim good news to the poor.*
> *He has sent me to heal the broken hearted,*
> *to preach deliverance to the captives and*
> *recovering of sight to the blind,*
> *to set a liberty those who are bruised."*
>
> *Luke 4:18*

Here we have the blueprint, God's design on how He is going to change you.

1. Firstly, *"He has anointed me to proclaim good news to the poor"*. This has first place of importance: telling people the gospel. The gospel is the 'good news' of the death and resurrection of our Saviour the Lord Jesus Christ. He gave His life for a propitiation for our sins.

The apostle John mentions the word "Propitiation" in the following passage,

> *"In this is love, not that we loved God, but*
> *that He loved us and sent His Son to be*
> *the propitiation for our sins"*
>
> *(1 John 4:10).*

This verse describes Christ's sacrificial death as the atonement for the sins that we have committed.

He loved us and gave His Son.

The good news is told to the poor. The poor are those who know their spiritual poverty and bereft state. They are sorry for their sins and for their inadequacies. This is good soil for the planting of the Word, the Word can be planted and develop good roots.

When the believer has repented of their sin, they are a new creation in Christ Jesus. The old has gone, the new had come.

Growing in Christ is taking hold of all that He has done for us on the Cross. He broke the power of Satan over our lives. He broke all the curses that came upon us through our fathers. With his stripes we are healed.

We can claim our inheritance as children of God, brothers and sisters of Jesus Christ.

2. Secondly, "*Jesus will heal the broken hearted*".

> *"Reproach has broken my heart*
> *and I am so sick. And I looked for*
> *sympathy, but there was none, and for*
> *comforters, but I found none."*
>
> *Psalm 69.20*

Who are the broken hearted? King David wrote the above lines. His life was fraught with difficulties, he had many enemies, one of which was his son, Absalom. Perhaps the reproach that he talks of here is when Nathan confronted him for taking Bathsheba, another man's wife, for himself. Then making sure the man was sent to a certain death on the front line of a battlefield.

His broken heart was caused by sin, it was 'sin sick', with no one to help. Perhaps he thought he was beyond redemption, many do, but Jesus has come to heal such a one.

He will heal those who have suffered incalculable loss. As a result of such loss many lose hope and become despairing. Jesus will come to that soul with a new hope and a new plan.

God's people were exiled to Babylon, taken many miles from their home with no expectation of returning. Lives were torn away from everything that was precious: homes, belongings, plans, work plans, even religious observances.

Daniel was among these people and God met his need. Daniel became a prominent member of the King's government and through Daniel's prayer life the King was blessed. God's name was honoured and glorified. God can bring wonderful things out of the ashes of destruction.

3.   Thirdly, "*preach deliverance to the captives*".

There are many people who are captive to destructive forces, this is both spiritual oppression from the enemy and oppression from fellow human beings. They have lived in darkness for a long time, their minds have been taken over, brain washed, they see things upside down and inside out. Their minds must be freed and retrained and turned to the truth.

Deliverance comes to those who are captive to the continual accusation from Satan, the enemy of God's people. Believers can now identify the difference between the whispering accusations from Satan that brings despair and the joy that comes from repentance. God does not bring despair, when this happens a believer can rest assured that that is the work of Satan.

4.   Fourthly, *"recover the sight of the blind"*.

Spiritual blindness will be removed, and the believer will see the truth. St Paul was blinded by God on the road to Damascus. This blindness was symbolic of his spiritual blindness that caused him to persecute Christians. God removed the blindness in a dramatic way. It is said it was like scales falling from his eyes. Then Paul was given the commission to preach 'Christ crucified' to the gentiles. This was a complete turn-around for Paul.

5.   Fifthly, *"to set at liberty those who are bruised"*.

To the world, a bruised reed is a worthless thing. It has no power, no stability, no purpose. It is good for nothing but to be cut down and discarded. So, in the world there are many bruised people, individuals who have been wounded emotionally, spiritually, or physically. They are feeble, and to most of the world, they are dispensable. But not to God. The prophecy of Isaiah (Isaiah 42:3) that Jesus fulfilled is that the bruised reed He would not break. It's a prophecy that speaks of Christ's tender, compassionate care for the weak and downtrodden.

The disfigured man whom Jesus met in Matthew 12 was a 'bruised reed', and Jesus gave him strength and cured his shrivelled hand. The woman taken in adultery was a 'bruised reed' in John 8 and Jesus saved her from stoning and forgave here sin. Jairus was a 'bruised reed' as he mourned his daughter's death, but Jesus strengthened his faith and raised his daughter from the dead. The woman with the issue of blood in Luke 8 was a 'bruised reed' and Jesus restored her to full health. The disciple Peter was a 'bruised reed' after his denial of the Lord, but Jesus gently and lovingly renewed him to fellowship after the resurrection. Over and over in the gospels, we see Jesus caring for the 'bruised reeds' of the world.

You may be a "bruised reed" in some way. You may be pressed down with the troubles of this world. You may be struggling with doubt and fear. You may be feeble and disheartened and ready to break. But know that Jesus cares. He will have pity for the broken-hearted, compassion for the humble, affection for the penitent, and healing for the afflicted. Come to Him in faith, humbly trusting His strength, and find that He is gracious to all.

Even although we go through these times of refining, and it can be very hard, we can rejoice that God loves us so much that He takes every sinful and painful part of us and lovingly makes us into vessels of honour.